Phonics Smart K·1

William Young • Janet Bartier

Love from Grandma

ISBN : 1-894810-85-6

Copyright © 2006 **Popular Book Company (Canada) Limited**

Printed in China

Contents

The Alphabet (1)

A. Trace the letters of the alphabet.

C. Some of the letters are not aboard the train. Help them out by writing the missing letters.

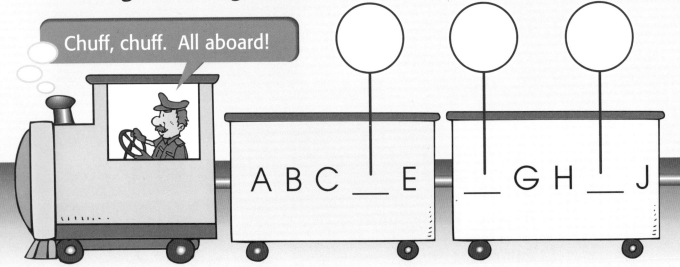

Chuff, chuff. All aboard!

A B C _ E   _ G H _ J

B. Make some noise by connecting the dots in alphabetical order.

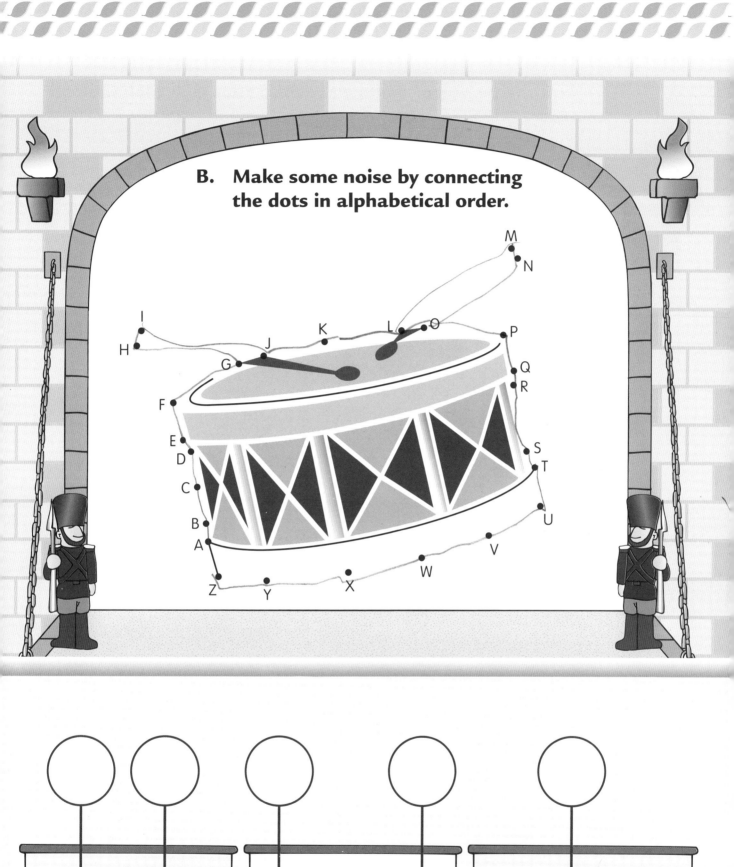

K __ M __ O   __ Q R S __   U V __ X Y Z

D. Find the treasure. Follow the path that is in alphabetical order.

A B C D B H K

A B J L

B F G M

E H I N

B C D I O

C D R Q P

D Q S G

V S

F U T S

G W V V

G Z

H V

I W

J X Y Z

E. Find and circle ◯ the letters hidden in this playground.

A. **What can you do with a sandy beach and a stick? Trace the lowercase letters in the sand.**

a b c d e f g h i

j k l m n o p q r

s t u v w x y z

C. **Someone's eaten the noodle letters! Write the missing letters in the spaces in alphabetical order.**

a _ c _ e   f _ h i _

B. Write the lowercase letter above its matching uppercase letter.

A B C D E F G H

I J K L M N O P Q

R S T U V W X Y Z

l n

p r t

v w y

D. Each set of footprints form a lowercase letter. Write the four letters that follow it in alphabetical order.

1.

2.

3.

E. The things in each planet all have the same beginning sound. Circle ○ the letter that gives them the sound.

Beginning Consonants (1)

A. Circle ◯ the food that begins with Mm in red and the animals that begin with Ss in blue.

B. Draw lines to match the pictures with the beginning letter Bb or Cc.

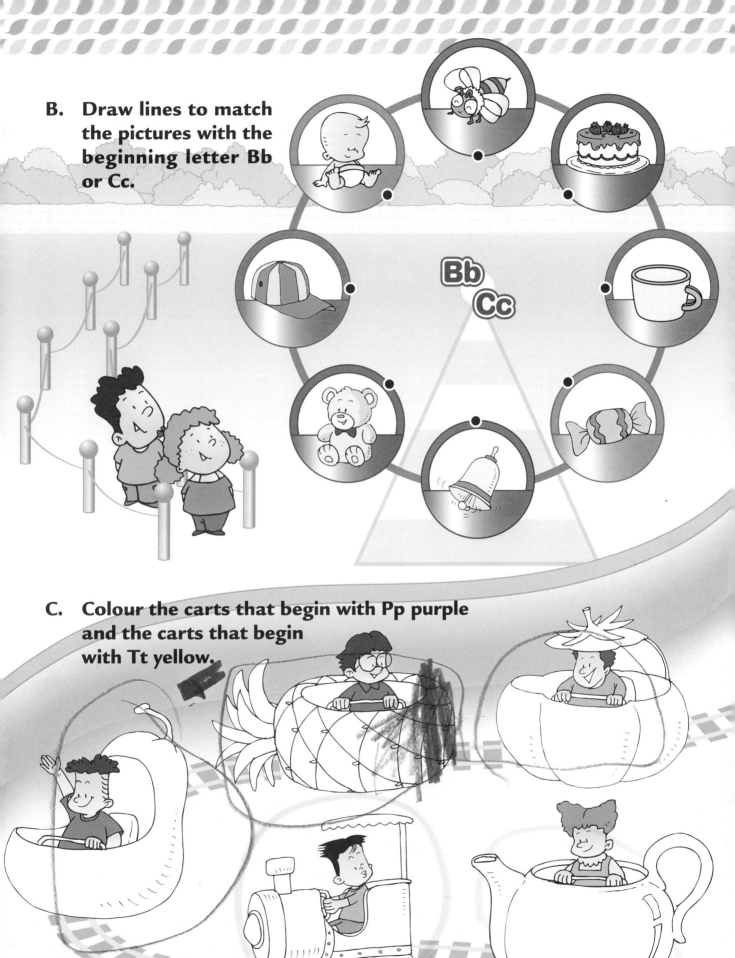

C. Colour the carts that begin with Pp purple and the carts that begin with Tt yellow.

D. The first letter is missing! Does the word begin with "d" or "f"? Write the correct letter at the beginning of each word.

1. ___ an

2. ___ lag

3. ___ uck

4. ___ oll

5. ___ ire

6. ___ art

7. ___ ox

8. ___ rum

9. ___ ish

E. Look at the pictures in each balloon. Say what they are. Cross out X the one that does not begin with the letter shown.

Beginning Consonants (2)

A. Words that begin with Vv go in the van. Words that begin with Ww go in the wagon. Write the numbers in the circles.

B. What sound does each picture begin with? Print the letter "h" or "z" to complete the words.

1. __ ebra

2. __ at

3. __ ipper

4. __ ero

5. __ elicopter

6. __ orse

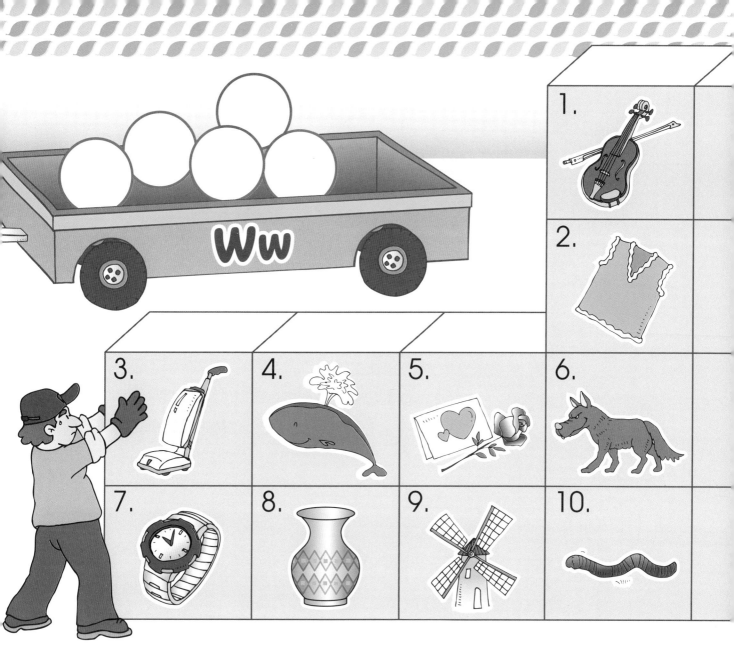

1.

2.

3.

4.

5.

6.

7.

8.

9.

10.

Ww

C. Say what the pictures are. Print the letter "y" if they begin with the Yy sound. Print the letter "n" if they begin with the Nn sound.

D. Colour the pictures that begin with the Ll sound.

E. Does it begin with Jj or Kk? Draw a line to join each picture to its matching card.

Beginning Consonants (3)

A. **Look at each picture. Colour the letter that begins the name of the object.**

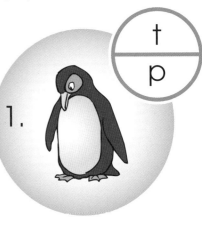

1.

t

p

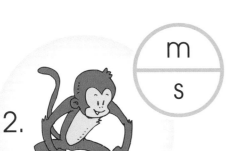

m

s

2.

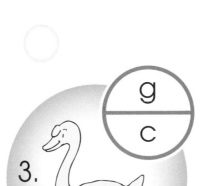

g

c

3.

f

v

4.

s

z

5.

6.

y

d

7.

l

n

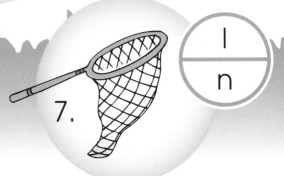

B. Join the children's lines with what they get.

C. The animals had T-shirts made that show their beginning sounds. Say what each animal is. Match each animal with its T-shirt by writing the letter in the box.

k

s

h

l

d

r

t

Get your own T-shirt.

m

D. Look at the way the children are moving. Print the first letter to finish the word that describes how each child moves.

1. __ alk

2. __ un

3. __ op

4. __ ie

5. __ rawl

6. __ wim

7. __ ump

Ending Consonants

A. Circle ○ the letter that ends the name of the thing that each shape looks like.

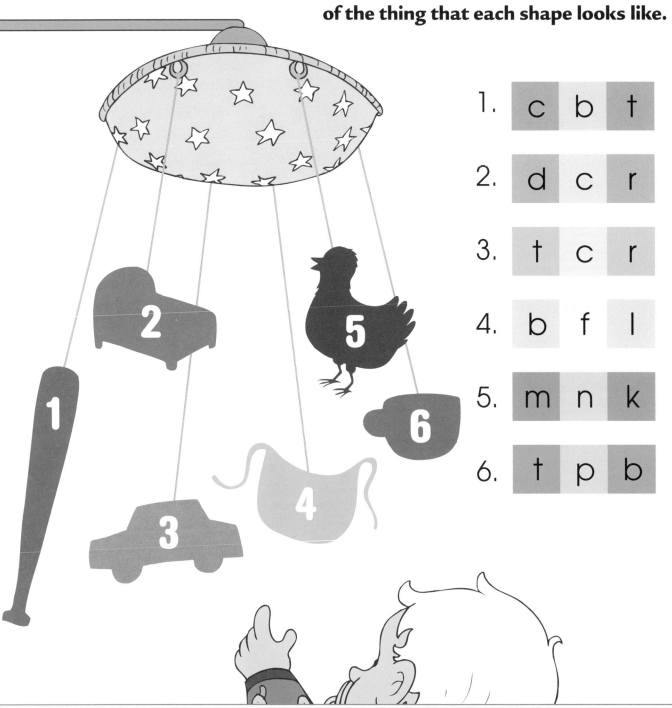

1. c b t

2. d c r

3. t c r

4. b f l

5. m n k

6. t p b

B. Look at the pictures. Write the letter that ends the name of each object.

1.

2.

3.

4.

5.

6.

7.

8.

9.

C. Complete each sign with the correct letter(s).

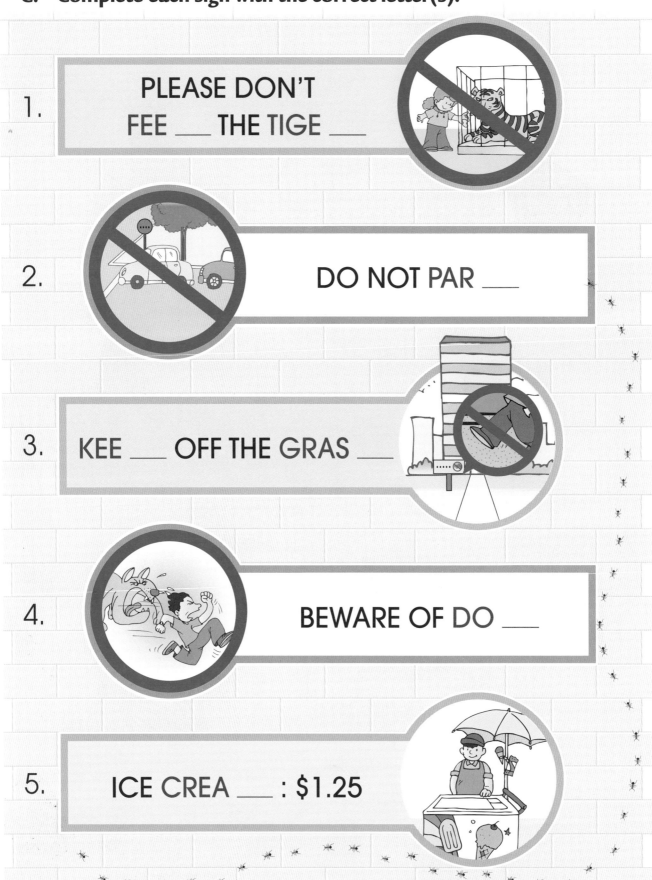

1. PLEASE DON'T FEE ___ THE TIGE ___

2. DO NOT PAR ___

3. KEE ___ OFF THE GRAS ___

4. BEWARE OF DO ___

5. ICE CREA ___ : $1.25

D. Complete the words in each group with the correct ending letters.

In each group, the first two words have the same ending letter. The last word has a different ending letter.

b m g t r n d

1.
fro __
ba __
car __

2.
lio __
ru __
ra __

3.
ca __
ba __
dru __

4.
ca __
doo __
bea __

5.
ha __
swi __
bir __

6.
cra __
ru __
shee __

7.
sin __
swin __
pin __

8.
po __
spo __
ja __

9.
han __
moo __
spoo __

Short Vowel "A"

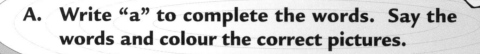

A. Write "a" to complete the words. Say the
words and colour the correct pictures.

1
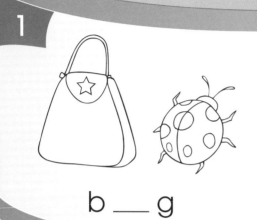
b __ g

2

c __ p

3

f __ n

4
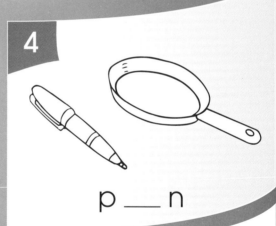
p __ n

5

h __ t

6

t __ p

B. Write the correct word under each picture. Match the words that rhyme.

cat   man   cap   can   mad

sad   tap   mat

C. Read the words. Write the letters in the correct boxes.

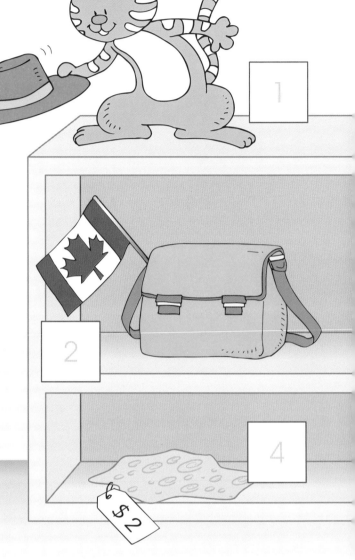

A. a rat and a bat

B. a hat and a cat

C. a flag and a bag

D. a tag and a rag

Smart *Practice*

How many words can you make with the short "a", using these letters?

_____

_____

_____

D. Help Anna get to her friend Lana. To make a path, draw lines to connect the words with the short "a" sound.

Anna

hand

dog

pan

mask

truck

bus

rake

crab

sun

fish

Lana

sack

sand

bat

pen

Short Vowel "E"

A. Print the letter "e" to finish each word. Say the word and draw a line to match it with the right picture.

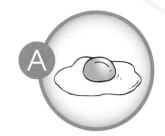
A

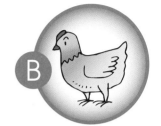
B

1. j __ t •

2. b __ d •

C

3. __ gg •

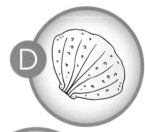
D

4. t __ nt •

5. h __ n •

E

6. r __ d •

F

7. sh __ ll •

G

8. sl __ d •

H

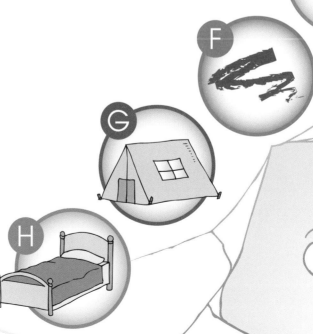

B. Colour the pictures that have a short "e". Print "e" to finish each word.

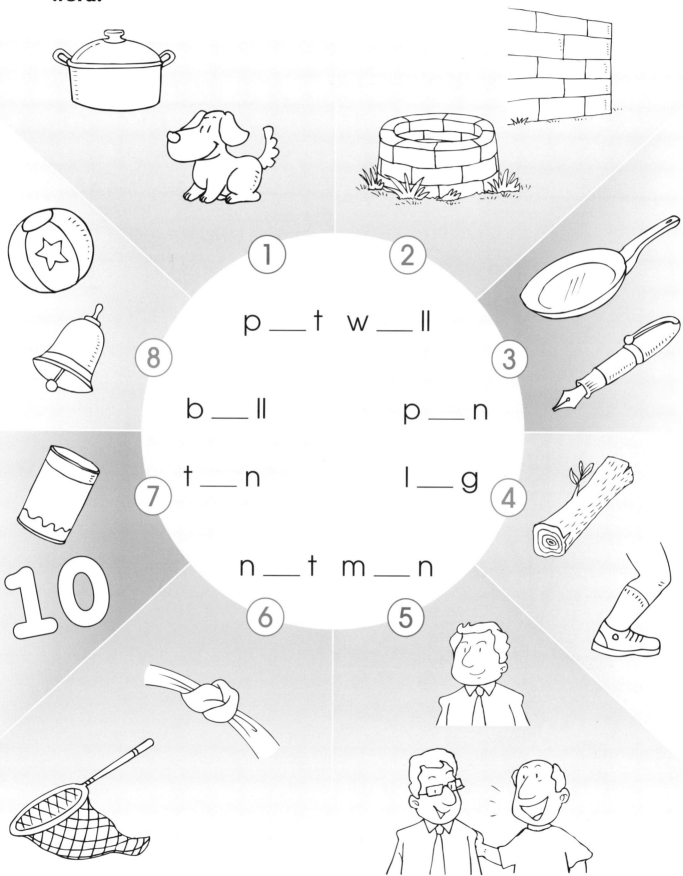

1. p __ t
2. w __ ll
3. p __ n
4. l __ g
5. m __ n
6. n __ t
7. t __ n
8. b __ ll

C. Use the letters from the lid to make words that rhyme.

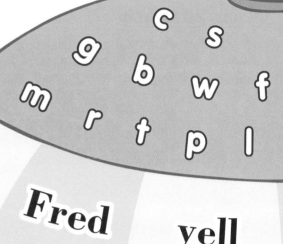

wet

___ et

___ et

___ et

___ et

___ et

___ et

Fred

___ ed

___ ed

___ ed

___ ed

___ ed

___ ed

yell

___ ell

___ ell

___ ell

___ ell

___ ell

___ ell

Smart *Practice*

Choose three of the following words to complete the funny sentence. Draw a picture to go with it.

sell   well
bell   fell   shell

The _____ _____ into the _____ .

D. **Help Spider Ted get to his web. Circle ◯ the things that have a short "e".**

Short Vowel "I"

A. Write "i" to complete each word. Match it with the picture by writing the letter in the spinner.

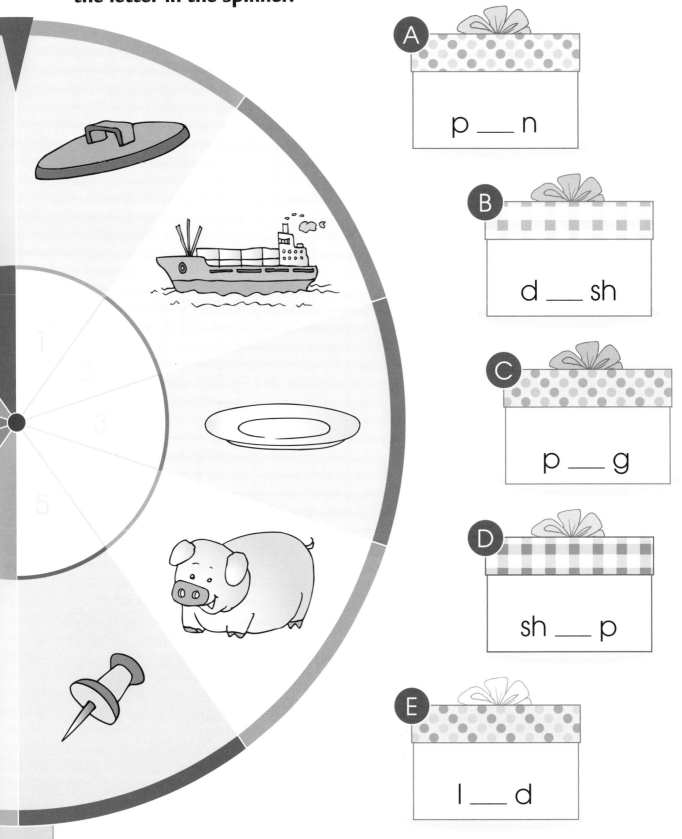

A p __ n

B d __ sh

C p __ g

D sh __ p

E l __ d

B. Print the letter "i" to finish each wish.

1. I wish for a f ___ sh.

2. I wish for a
    k ___ ss.

3. I wish for a
    h ___ t.

Best Wishes

4. I wish for a
    m ___ tt.

5. I wish for a sh ___ p.

C. In each group of pictures, colour the one that has the short "i" sound.

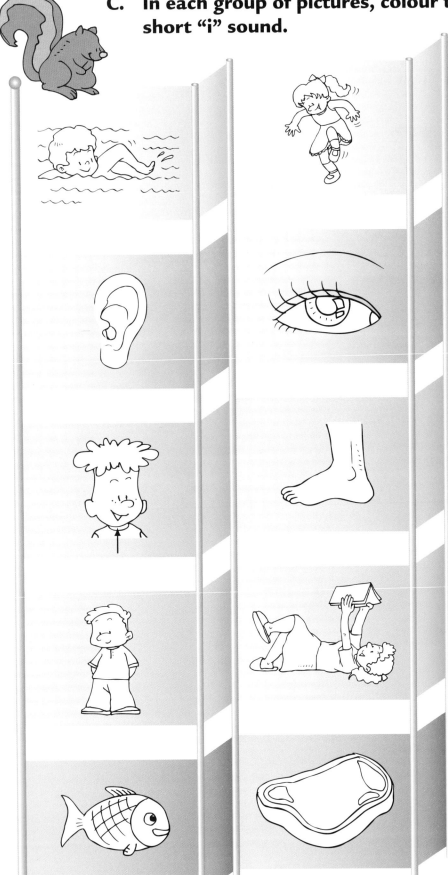

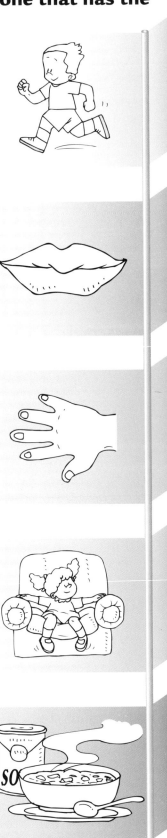

D. Use the beginning sounds on the bridge to make words that rhyme with "it" and "hip".

f   l   p   b   t   r   w   s   d   z

it   hip

_____   _____

_____   _____

_____   _____

_____   _____

Smart Practice

Complete the sentence with these words. Draw a picture to go with it.

big   wig   pig

The _____ is

wearing a _____

_____ .

Short Vowel "O"

A. Draw lines to join the things that have a short "o" sound to the box.

The word "box" has a short "o" sound.

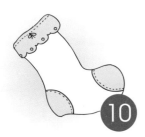

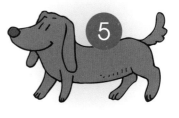

B. **Put the letters in the correct order. Write each word under the right picture.**

pmo
otp
poh
tho
opt

1. _____

2. _____

3. _____

4. _____

5. _____

C. Say the name of each thing. Colour the two that rhyme.

1.

2.

3.

4.

Smart Practice

Choose three words to complete the funny sentence. Draw a picture to go with it.

fox   box

pot   dog   sock

The _____ in the

_____ is wearing

a _____ .

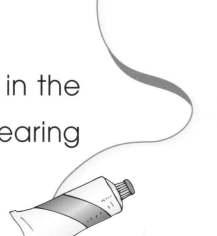

D. Print the correct description beside each picture.

Welcome to the Short "o" Art Gallery

Lots of dots
Soft socks
An ox on a rock
A hopping dog

1. _____

2. _____

3. _____

4. _____

Short Vowel "U"

A. Finish each word in the mug with the letter "u". Match the word with the right picture. Write the letter in the circle.

A. tr __ ck

B. b __ g

C. d __ ck

D. m __ ffin

E. b __ n

F. s __ n

B.   Be a magician. Change the vowel to "u" to make a new word. Say the word.

1. h o g ➡ h ⬜ g

2. j i g ➡ j ⬜ g

3. r e s t ➡ r ⬜ s t

4. h a t ➡ h ⬜ t

5. f i n ➡ f ⬜ n

6. b i n ➡ b ⬜ n

7. r i g ➡ r ⬜ g

8. t a c k ➡ t ⬜ c k

9. j e s t ➡ j ⬜ s t

10. p a c k ➡ p ⬜ c k

C. What do they say? Draw lines to match the words with the right pictures.

- Yuck!

- Ruff, ruff!

- Chuff, chuff!

- Run, run as fast as you can.

- I'll huff and I'll puff...

- Yum, yum!

Smart Practice

Write these four words in the blanks to make a silly sentence. Draw a picture to go with it.

bug   rug
tug   slug

A _____

and a _____

_____ on a

_____ .

D. Say the name of each thing. Colour the two that rhyme.

Short Vowels

A. **Say what the animals are. Print the missing letter for each animal.**

b __ t

p __ g

h __ n

d __ ck

sk __ nk

f __ x

__ l __ phant

cr __ b

f __ sh

fr __ g

B. **Say what each picture is. For each block, colour the two that have the same short vowel sound.**

C. Finish the silly rhyme by printing the vowels that fit.

a f ___ x throwing r ___ cks?

a b ___ t wearing a h ___ t?

a f ___ sh making a w ___ sh?

a cl ___ ck wearing a s ___ ck?

a p ___ t flying a j ___ t?

a b ___ g drinking from a m ___ g?

a h ___ n counting to t ___ n?

a d ___ g going for a j ___ g?

Did you ever see . . .

What vowel completes these three words?

They are all animal homes.

n ___ st   w ___ b   sh ___ ll

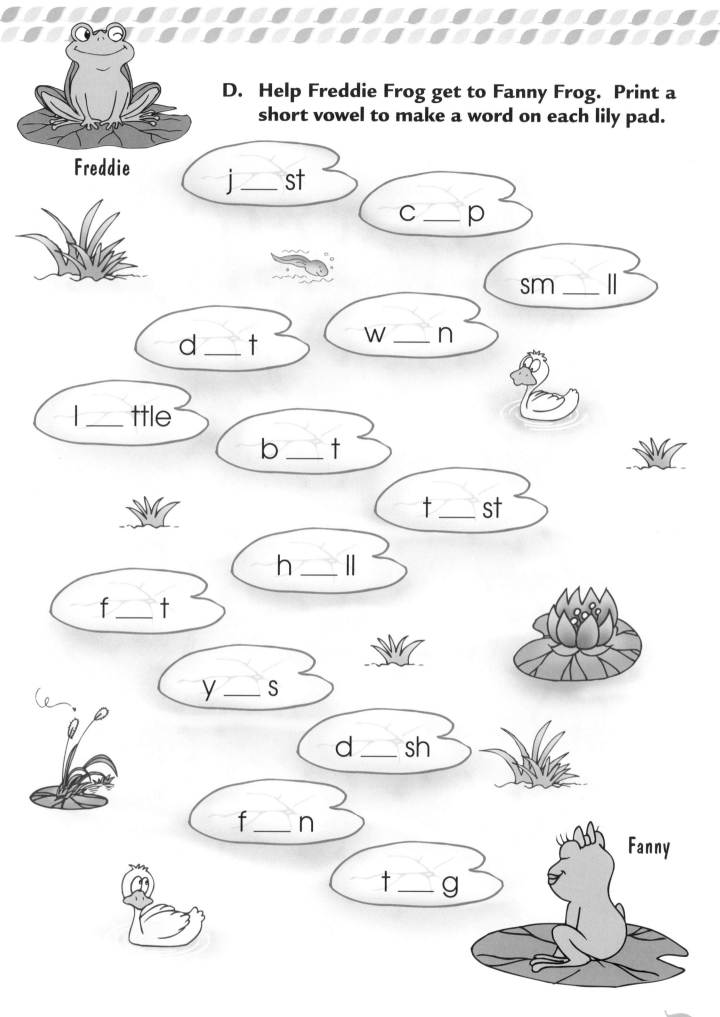

D. Help Freddie Frog get to Fanny Frog. Print a short vowel to make a word on each lily pad.

Freddie

j __ st

c __ p

sm __ ll

d __ t

w __ n

l __ ttle

b __ t

t __ st

h __ ll

f __ t

y __ s

d __ sh

f __ n

t __ g

Fanny

A. Help Derek tidy up his things. Draw a line from each thing to its beginning letter.

1.

2.

3.

4.

5.

6.

7.

8.

9.

C. Write the beginning consonant of each thing in the ◯ and the ending consonant in the ⬡.

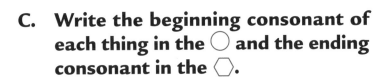

1.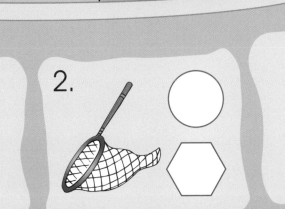

2.

3.

4.

5.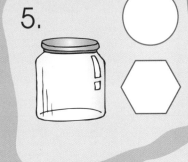

6.

7.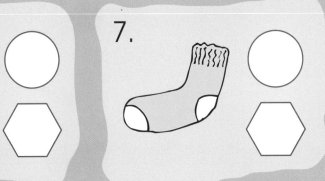

8.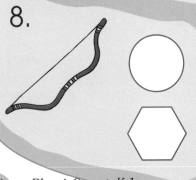

9.

10.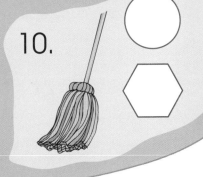

D. Circle ⭕ the correct short vowels to complete the words.

1.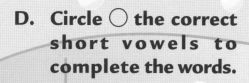
sh | a | e | ll

2.
st | i | a | r

3.
r | i | u | ng

4.
f | a | o | x

5.
sh | i | o | p

6.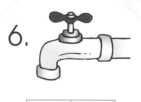
t | i | a | p

7.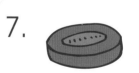
p | a | u | ck

8.
t | a | o | p

9.
v | a | e | st

10.
j | i | u | g

fin

tag

bag

chin

smell

mitt

box

tell

hit

ox

E. Read the words on the left. Write
them next to the correct rhyming words.

flag   _____   _____

well   _____   _____

fit   _____   _____

pin   _____

        _____

fox   _____

        _____

F. Put the letters in order. Draw a line to match each word with the right picture.

a b t

b _ _ _ •

s i h f

_ _ i _ _ •

o l k c

l _ _ _ _ •

u t b

_ _ _ b •

a r c

_ a _ •

e l l b

_ _ _ l •

Long Vowels / Silent "E"

A. Say the long "a" words. Draw lines to match the words with the pictures.

shave •

cake •

rake •

whale •

ape •

gate •

game •

tape •

lake •

B. **Help Nate add the silent "e" to make long "a" words. Say the words.**

1. fat _____

2. cap _____

3. fad _____

4. hat _____

5. tap _____

6. mad _____

7. rat _____

8. bath _____

9. pal _____

10. at _____

C. Colour the pictures that have the long "i" sound.

D. Add the silent "e" to make long "i" words.

1. kit _____ 2. bit _____

3. pin _____ 4. fin _____

5. rip _____ 6. pip _____

7. rid _____ 8. hid _____

E. **Choose the long "o" words that end in the silent "e" from the signpost to finish these rhymes.**

1. Go up a slope
   Using a _____

2. Water the rose
   Using a _____

3. Carry the globe
   Wearing your _____

4. Bury the bone
   Under the _____

rope   hole
stone
robe   hose

5. Look at the mole
   Digging a _____

More Long Vowels / Silent "E"

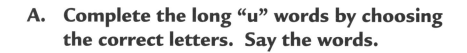

A. Complete the long "u" words by choosing the correct letters. Say the words.

j p c m r t

1. __ ure   2. __ une

3. __ ule   4. __ ure

5. __ une

6. __ ule

B. Add the silent "e" to make long "u" words. Say the new words.

1. dud __   2. cub __

3. hug __   4. cut __

5. tub __   6. us __

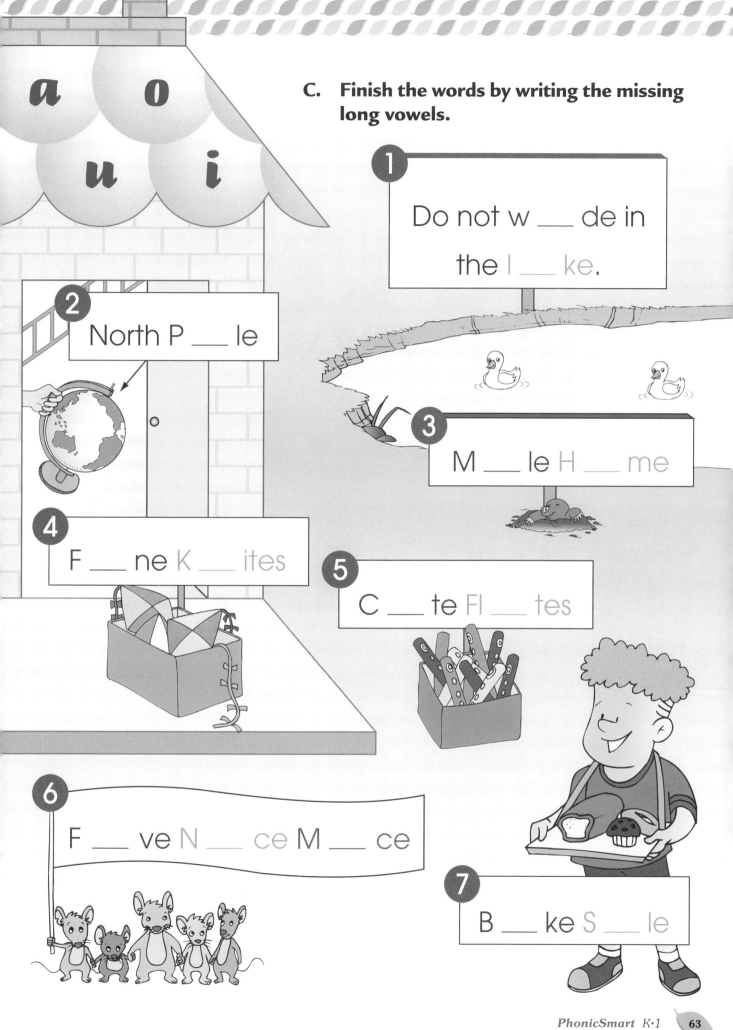

a o u i

C. **Finish the words by writing the missing long vowels.**

1 Do not w __ de in the l __ ke.

2 North P __ le

3 M __ le H __ me

4 F __ ne K __ ites

5 C __ te Fl __ tes

6 F __ ve N __ ce M __ ce

7 B __ ke S __ le

D. A new vowel has been given to each word. Use the letter to make a new word.

cane

ripe

mile

mole

bike

fume

rode

role

pale

wrote

o — c __ ne

o — r __ pe

a — m __ le

u — m __ le

a — b __ ke

a — f __ me

i — r __ de

u — r __ le

o — p __ le

i — wr __ te

E. Choose the words from the sign to complete the puzzle.

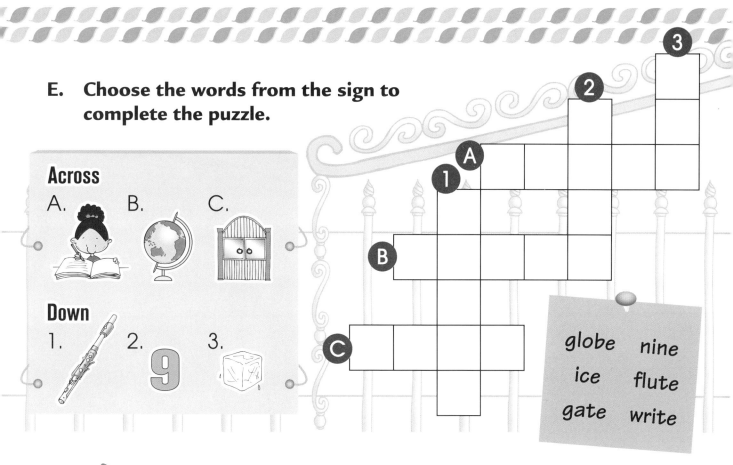

Across

A. B. C.

Down

1. 2. **9** 3.

globe nine
ice flute
gate write

Smart *Practice*

Draw a line to match each child with the thing that has the same long vowel.

Luke
Jane
Joe
Mike

Consonant Blends "L"

These words have two beginning consonants.

A. Say what each picture is. Colour the circle with the "l" blend that begins each word.

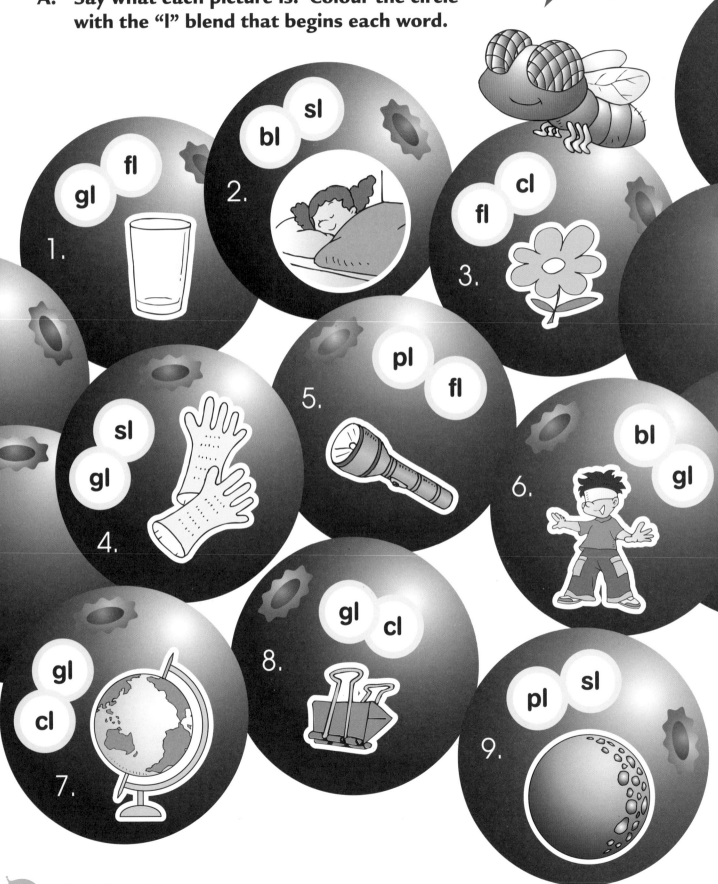

10. sl / bl

11. sl / cl

12. cl / pl

13. gl / pl

14. bl / fl

15. sl / fl

16. cl / bl

B. Put each group of letters in the correct blank to form a word with the "l" blend.

1. bl _____   2. cl _____

3. fl _____   4. gl _____

5. pl _____   6. sl _____

ove am
ant ag
oom ug

C. **For each group, choose from the blends to make words that rhyme. Say the rhyming words.**

bl
pl   cl
fl   gl
sl

_____ ock

1.   _____ ock   _____ ock

2.   _____ ue   _____ ue   _____ ue

3.   _____ ow   _____ ow   _____ ow

4.   _____ ip   _____ ip   _____ ip

5.   _____ ot   _____ ot

_____ ot

D. For each group of pictures, cross out X the one that has a different beginning blend.

1.

2.

3.

4.

5.

6.

Consonant Blends "R"

A. Read the poem. Underline the words that begin with an "r" blend.

Brenda and Fred

Dreamed of fresh bread

So they grabbed a train to get some

But the train drove back

(There was a crack in the track)

And our friends did not get a crumb

B. Circle ◯ a blend to make new words to rhyme with the words shown by the pictures.

cr		br		fr		dr	
tr	eam	pr	ain	gr	ove	cr	ead

C. Say the tongue-twisters out loud. Colour the "r" blend words in the word search.

> Bricks break brown bread.
> Find fresh fruit for Frank.
> Greta grows great grapes.

e	s	w	g	p	w	n	u					b
	k	m	G	o	w	r		s	d	b	u	i
b		B	r	i	c	k	s		F	r	c	t
r	y	n	e	a	n		a	t		o	r	F
	a	F	t	e			i	b	r	w	G	r
k	g	r	a	p	e	s	B	r		n	c	a
	r		e		f	r	e	s	h		t	n
j	a	c	s	h	r	c		a	p	B	i	k
p	e	y	m	b	s	g	b	d			s	n
l	f	e	g	r	o	w	s	t	w		o	p
	s	f		e	i	c	a	k	b	a	h	e
h	g	r	e	a	t	a		f	r	u	i	t
a	c	e	r	k	s	p		w	i	e	s	n

D. Choose the blend that begins each word.

br	cr	dr
fr	gr	pr	tr

1.

_____ ess

2.

_____ ead

3.

_____ ain

4.

_____ og

5.

_____ apes

6.

_____ own

7.

_____ uck

8.

_____ um

9.
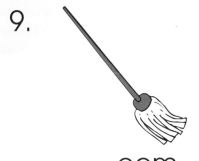
_____ oom

10.
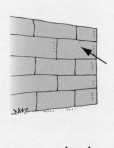
_____ ick

11.

_____ ab

12.
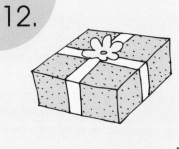
_____ esent

E. Help Chris Crab get to Christa Crab. Draw a path by connecting the pictures with an "r" blend.

Consonant Blends "S"

A. Choose the correct "s" blend from the mushroom stem for each of these pictures.

1. _____ arf

3. _____ rew

2. _____ im

4. _____ ar

7. _____ unk

5. _____ ake

6. _____ ile

9. _____ ow

8. _____ oon

sw st sp
sn sm sk sc

B. Read the word above each pair of pictures. Circle ○ the picture that matches the word.

1. speed

2. ski

3. swing

4. stand

5. snail

6. school

C. Print the word endings to make these rhyming words. Say the words.

1. **in**

sk _____
sp _____

2. **an**

sc _____
sp _____

3. **all**

st _____
sm _____

4. **ow**

sn _____
st _____

5. **y**

sk _____
sp _____

6. **ell**

sm _____
sp _____

7. **ip**

sn _____
sk _____

8. **im**

sk _____
sw _____

9. **oop**

sc _____
sn _____

10. **ill**

st _____
sp _____

D. Spot the "s" blends. Circle ◯ the pictures with an "s" blend sound.

1.

2.

3.

4.

5.

6.

7.

8.

9.

Consonant Blends - Review

A. Find pictures with the same beginning blends. Colour them with the same colour. Use a different colour for each pair.

B. Write the beginning blend that goes with each picture.

1.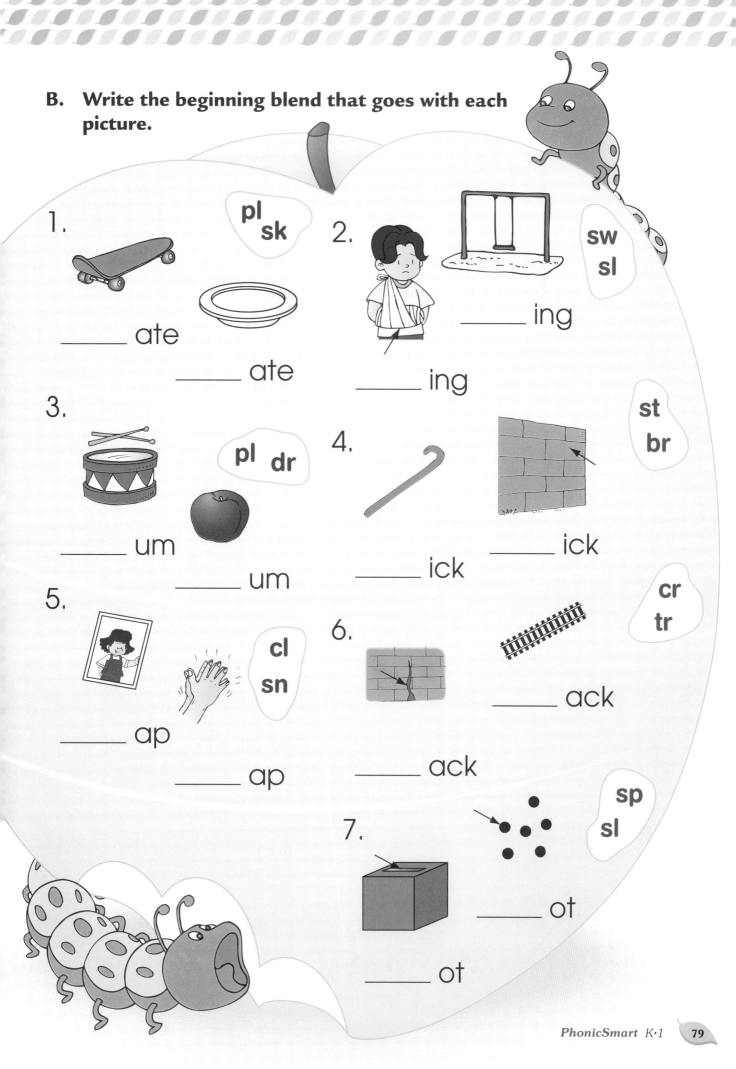

pl
sk

____ ate

____ ate

2.

sw
sl

____ ing

____ ing

3.

pl dr

____ um

____ um

4.

st
br

____ ick

____ ick

5.

cl
sn

____ ap

____ ap

6.

cr
tr

____ ack

____ ack

7.

sp
sl

____ ot

____ ot

C. The blends in these words are in the wrong places! Switch the blends to make them right. The first one is done for you.

1. flowsnake   ___sn___ ow ___fl___ ake

2. tream stain   _____ eam _____ ain

3. trimb a clee   _____ imb a _____ ee

4. steak a brick   _____ eak a _____ ick

5. tray a plick   _____ ay a _____ ick

6. drog a clain   _____ og a _____ ain

7. ply a flane   _____ y a _____ ane

8. gloken brass   _____ oken _____ ass

9. snow as a slail

   _____ ow as a _____ ail

10. flell a smower

   _____ ell a _____ ower

D. Write the blend that fits the beginning of each word. Say the word.

sc

tr st gr

fl cl fr

sm bl

pl

1. _____ ower

2. _____ ock

3. _____ ain

4. _____ ile

5. _____ own

6. _____ ant

7. _____ ar

8. _____ ock

9. _____ apes

10. _____ arf

11. _____ unk

12. _____ ute

13. _____ oud

Consonant Digraphs "CH" and "SH"

A.   Check ✔ the pictures that begin with "ch".

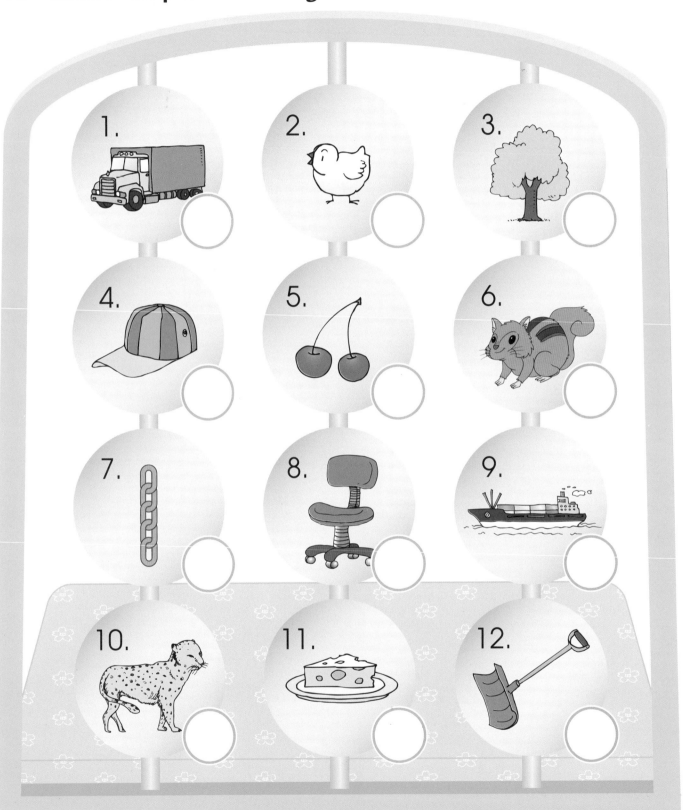

1.

2.

3.

4.

5.

6.

7.

8.

9.

10.

11.

12.

B. Finish the words by adding "sh". Match the words with the right pictures by writing the numbers under the pictures.

1. ____ ell

2. di ____

3. ____ ark

4. ____ irt

5. ____ awl

6. tra ____

7. ____ ave

8. bru ____

9. ____ ower

10. ____ adow

C. Use "sh" or "ch" to make a word that rhymes with each of these words.

mill

1. _____ ill

sat

2. _____ at

brave

3. _____ ave

be

4. _____ e

sell

5. _____ ell

seek

6. _____ eek

neck

7. _____ eck

lime

8. _____ ime

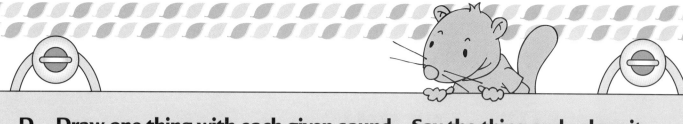

D. Draw one thing with each given sound. Say the thing and colour it.

Beginning: "ch" sound

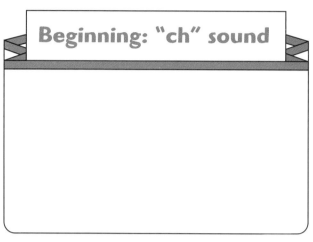

Ending: "ch" sound

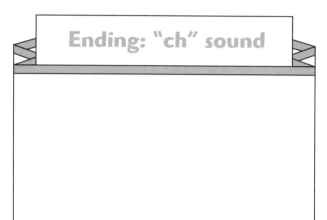

Beginning: "sh" sound

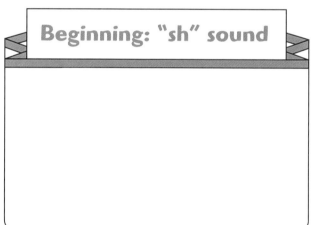

Ending: "sh" sound

Smart *Practice*

Write a word that has the "ch" sound at the beginning and at the end.

Some people go there on Sundays.

_ _ _ _ _ _ _ _

Consonant Digraphs "TH" and "WH"

A. Finish the words by adding "th". Match them with the pictures.

1. ____ umb •

2. pa ____ •

3. ____ row •

4. ____ ink •

5. ba ____ •

B. Find and circle these common "th" words in the word search.

the   them

those   there

this   that

they

e	o	t	h	e	y	t
m	t	h	o	s	e	a
t	h	e	m	r	t	m
h	a	r	y	e	h	r
e	t	e	t	h	i	s

C. **Make the wheel go round by adding "wh" to each word ending. Say the word.**

1. ____ at

2. ____ en

3. ____ ite

4. ____ y

5. ____ ere

6. ____ ich

7. ____ ale

8. ____ ip

Smart Practice

Which words from (C) would be the questions to these answers?

1. _____ ?   Now.

2. _____ ?   At the park.

3. _____ ?   So we can play.

D. Use "th" or "wh" to make rhyming pairs.

1. bat

   _____ at

2. peel

   _____ eel

3. free

   _____ ree

4. ship

   _____ ip

5. my

   _____ y

6. stem

   _____ em

7. rich

   _____ ich

8. sing

   _____ ing

9. kite

   _____ ite

10. file

    _____ ile

Where?

There.

E. Circle ◯ the correct beginning for each of these pictures.

1. wh   th

2. wh   th

3. wh   th

4. **3** wh   th

5. wh   th

6. wh   th

7. wh   th

8. wh   th

9. wh   th

10. wh   th

11. wh   th

12. **1000** wh   th

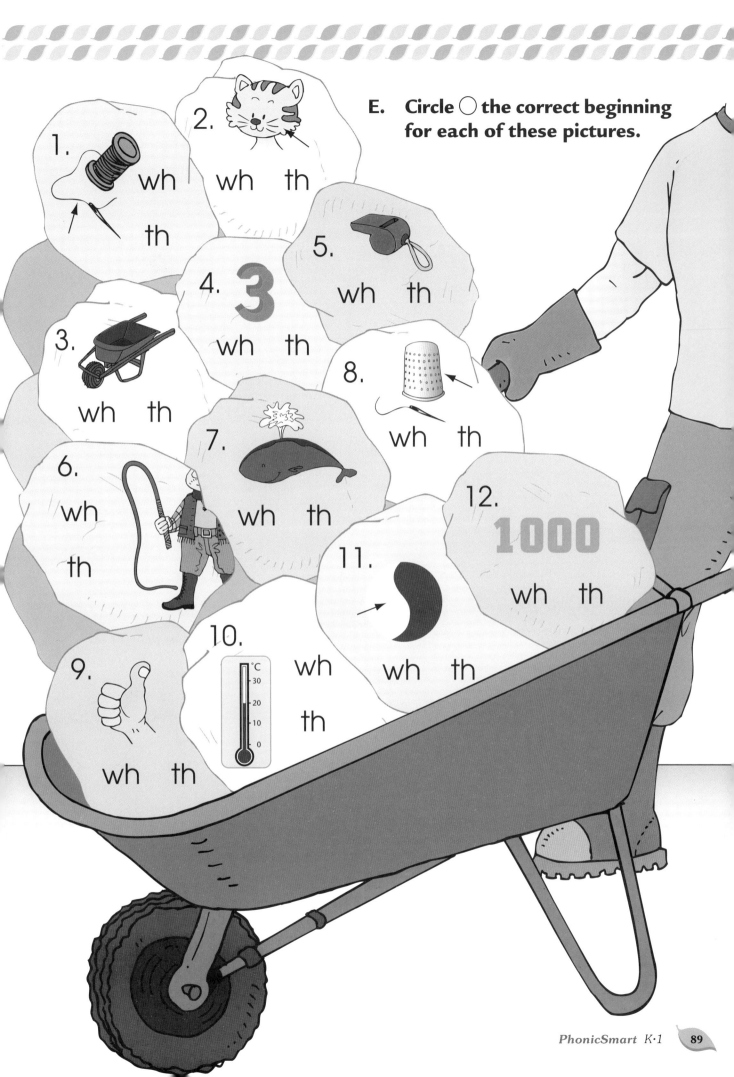

"ER", "IR", and "UR"

A. Complete the words by writing "er", "ir", or "ur". Match each word with its picture by colouring the picture with the colour of the word.

ER

1. swimm __er__

2. f ____ n

3. p ____ son

4. wat ____

5. h ____ d

6. moth ____

IR

1. g ____ l

2. sk ____ t

3. sh ____ t

4. b ____ d

5. c ____ cle

6. wh ____ l

UR

1. c _____ l

2. t _____ key

3. t _____ n

4. n _____ se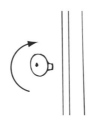

5. ch _____ ch

6. p _____ se

B. **Circle ◯ the pictures that have "er", "ir", or "ur".**

1.

2.

3.

4.

C. Read the verse. Write the "er", "ir", and "ur" words on the lines below. Do not repeat the same words.

Sir Burt and Sir Bernie were digging in dirt

When Sir Bernie got dirt on his shirt.

"That dirt on your shirt

Won't hurt," said Sir Burt.

"Here's water –

Just give it a squirt!"

D. Colour the animals that have "er", "ir", or "ur".

Vowel Pair "EE"

A. Circle ◯ the words in the poem that have "ee". Find the "ee" words in the poem that match the pictures.

Beep! Beep! Said the jeep.

Wheels peeling down the street.

Hush! Or wake the sheep we keep.

It's fast asleep and dreaming sweet.

1.

2.

3.

4.

5.

B. Look at the pictures. Finish the words by adding the right endings.

1.

tr _____

2.

qu _____

3.

b _____

4.

sw _____

5.

t _____

6.

wh _____

ee

eel

een

eet

eep

eeth

7.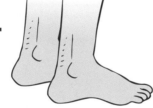

f _____

8.

sh _____

9.

p _____

10.

sh _____

C. Check ✔ the one in each pair that has an "ee" sound in it.

1.

2.

3.

4.

5.

6.

7.

8.

D. **Finish the silly questions by adding "ee" to make rhyming words.**

1. Did you ever see g _____ se eating ch _____ se?

2. Did you ever see an _____ l eating a p _____ l?

3. Did you ever put a wh _____ l on your h _____ l?

4. Did you ever see a s _____ d talking to a r _____ d?

5. Did you ever see a b _____ climbing up a tr _____ ?

E. **Cross out ✗ one word in each group that does not have the "ee" sound.**

1. see   we   wet

2. key   bee   bed

3. pear   eat   seed

4. deer   dear   wear

5. he   she   pet

6. feel   eel   sell

Vowel Pair "OO"

A. Finish the animal words by writing "oo". Help
    Judy print the animal names in the boxes.

kangar _____

racc _____ n

cuck _____

l _____ n

r _____ ster

bab _____ n

g _____ se

m _____ se

1.

2.

3.

4.

5.

6.

B. Write the letters in the ⬜ **to show the sounds they make.**

A moo   **B** hoot   **C** shoo

D woof   **E** boo   **F** zoom

G cock-a-doodle-doo

1

2

3

4

5

6

7

C. Circle ○ the words that match the pictures.

1. book
   boot

2. noon
   moon

3. balloon
   baboon

4. broom
   bloom

5. food
   flood

6. roof
   hoof

7. hood
   hook

8. wool
   wood

D. Complete the words that rhyme with the first word in each hoop. Say the words.

1. hoop

   sc _____

   sn _____

   l _____

2. pool

   sch _____

   c _____

   f _____

3. root

   sh _____

   b _____

   l _____

4. book

   c _____

   h _____

   l _____

5. zoo

   sh _____

   m _____

   b _____

6. broom

   bl _____

   b _____

   r _____

"Y" as a Vowel

"Y" can make a long "e" sound as it does in the word "rainy".

A. Look at each picture. Write the correct word under the picture.

1
2
3
4
5
6
7
8
9
10
11
12

snowy	city	curly
cherry	lady	rocky
happy	baby	sunny
starry	jelly	marry

B.   Read the words. Circle ◯ the sound the "y" makes.

1. shy   long "i"   long "e"

2. sorry   long "i"   long "e"

3. July   long "i"   long "e"

4. spy   long "i"   long "e"

5. only   long "i"   long "e"

6. dry   long "i"   long "e"

7. pretty   long "i"   long "e"

8. body   long "i"   long "e"

9. lazy   long "i"   long "e"

10. dye   long "i"   long "e"

11. cry   long "i"   long "e"

12. buddy   long "i"   long "e"

13. my   long "i"   long "e"

14. every   long "i"   long "e"

"Y" can make a long "i" sound as it does in the word "fly".

C. For each pair of pictures, circle ◯ the one that uses "y" as a vowel.

1. berry   yo-yo

2. bye-bye   yellow

3. cry   yawn

4. yarn   dye

5. yolk   shiny

6. family   yard

7. shy   yell

8. yak   jelly

D. Add a "y" to each word and draw a line to join it to the right picture.

1. dais ___ •

2. pupp ___ •

3. sk ___ •

4. bab ___ •

5. pon ___ •

6. penn ___ •

7. bunn ___ •

8. cherr ___ •

Smart *Practice*

Finish the words by adding the "y" with the long "i" sound.

Wh ___ did the hungry frog cr ___?

He missed the fl ___ when it flew b ___ .

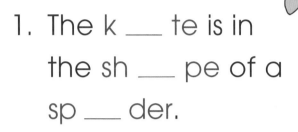

A. Fill in the blanks with long vowels to complete the sentences.

1. The k __ te is in the sh __ pe of a sp __ der.

2. Gladys keeps the m __ ce in a c __ ge.

3. The wh __ le is a h __ ge ocean animal.

4. There's a c __ ve by the l __ ke.

5. Mom has grown a lot of wh __ te r __ ses in front of the house.

6. Morris rushed h __ me to fetch his fl __ te.

7. You can __ se this r __ ler to measure the s __ des of the c __ be.

8. __ ce cream c __ nes are his favourite treats.

B. **Look at the pictures. Colour the ◯ with the correct beginning blends.**

1. dr

2. sk

3. sc

4. pl

5. pr

6. sl

7. cr

8. sw

9. fl

C. Print the correct consonant digraph for each picture.

1.
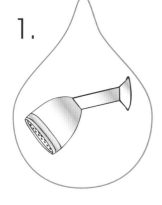

_____ ower

2.

_____ umb

3.
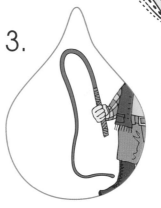

_____ ip

4.

_____ air

5.

_____ adow

6.

_____ ick

7.

_____ ree

8.
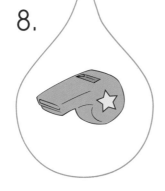

_____ istle

9.

_____ eel

ch

sh

th

wh

D. Match the "er", "ir", and "ur" words with the right pictures. Write the letters in the boxes.

A. toaster

B. twirl

C. shirt

D. flipper

E. turkey

F. thirst

G. fern

H. burr

I. hurt

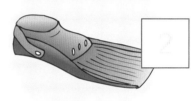

E. Write "oo" or "ee" to complete each word.

1.

t＿＿p＿＿

2.

f＿＿d

3.

w＿＿p

4.

fr＿＿＿

5.

st＿＿l

6.

h＿＿k

7.

＿＿l

8.

br＿＿m

9.

p＿＿l

F. Circle ◯ the words using "y" as a vowel. Write the words in the tree.

snowy

party

kayak   sky

happy   hay

baby   cry

try   dry

celery

birthday

pigsty

candy

monkey

butterfly

Long "i"

_____

_____

_____   _____

_____   _____

Long "e"

_____   _____

_____   _____

_____   _____

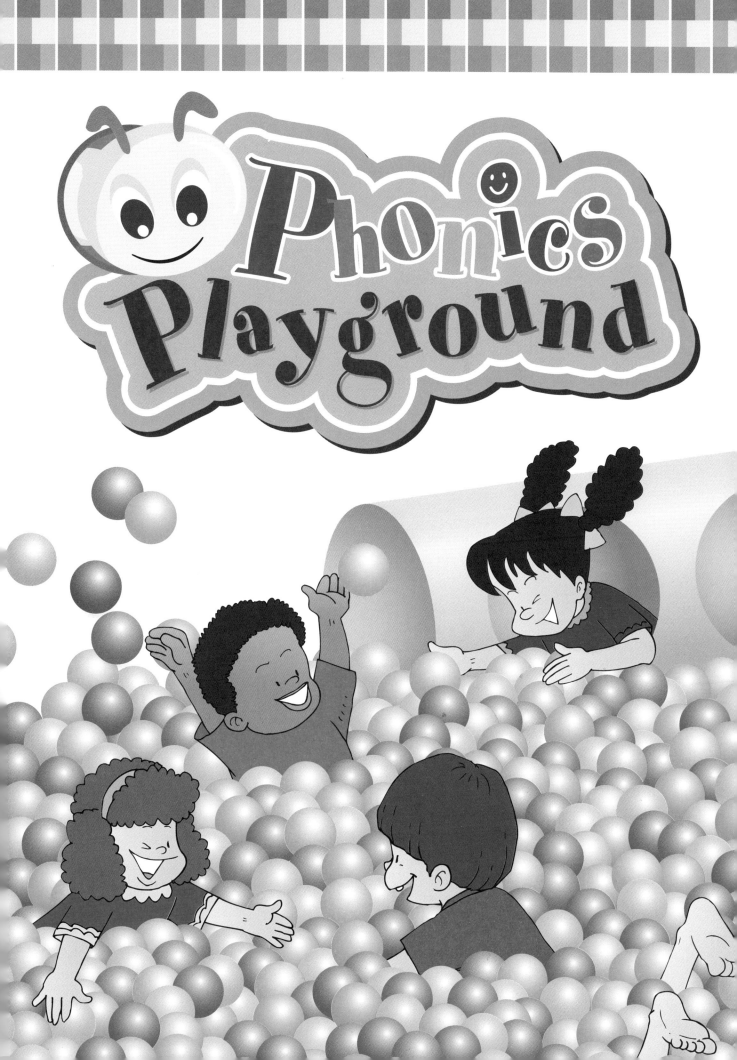

1

Draw the path that Benny Bear takes to get to the honey. Avoid all the vowels.

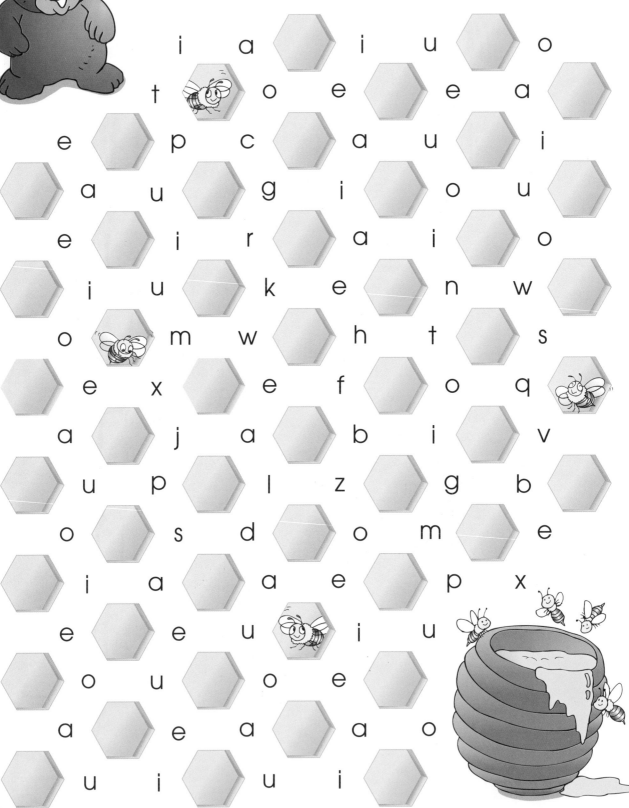

For each group of pictures, cross out X the picture that begins with a different sound from the others.

**Colour the pictures
with long vowels.**

4

Phonics Playground

Look at each picture. Fill in the missing vowel. Colour the ☆ if it is a short vowel; colour the ◇ if it is a long vowel.

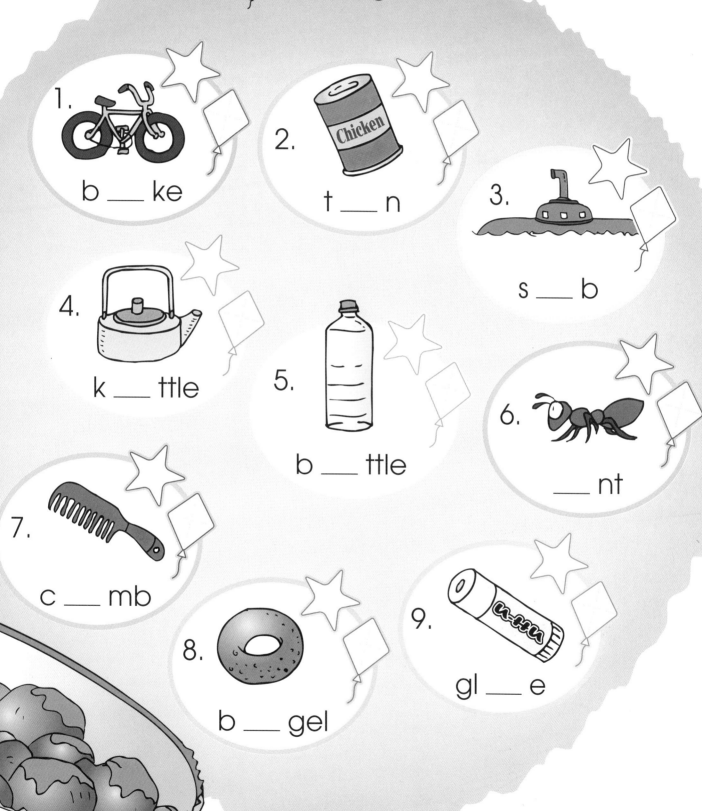

1. b __ ke

2. t __ n

3. s __ b

4. k __ ttle

5. b __ ttle

6. __ nt

7. c __ mb

8. b __ gel

9. gl __ e

5

Phonics Playground

Match the letters in the shooting stars with those on the planet to form words.

tw

pl

wh

sh

ch

cl

th

cr

sq

br

ich
ree
uare
oom
ayon
oud
anet
alk
ice
irt

6

Write four words that begin with each consonant blend.

sw

sn

tr

dr

cl

pl

1 The Alphabet (1)

B.

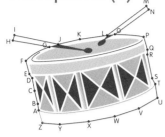

C. D ; F ; I ; L ; N ; P ; T ; W

D.

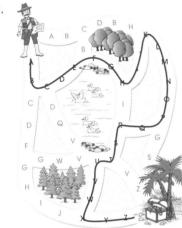

E.

2 The Alphabet (2)

B.

C. b ; d ; g ; j ; k ; m ; o ; q ; s ; u ; x ; z

D. 1. d ; e ; f ; g   2. m ; n ; o ; p

3. w ; x ; y ; z

E. 1. s   2. b   3. m
   4. d   5. r

3 Beginning Consonants (1)

A.

B.

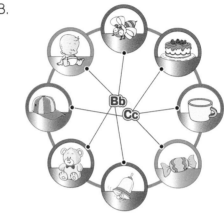

C.

D. 1. f   2. f   3. d
   4. d   5. f   6. d
   7. f   8. d   9. f

E. 1.   2.   3.
   4.   5.

4 Beginning Consonants (2)

A. Vv – 1 ; 2 ; 3 ; 5 ; 8   Ww – 4 ; 6 ; 7 ; 9 ; 10

B. 1. z   2. h   3. z
   4. z   5. h   6. h

C. y ; y ; n ; y ; n ; n

D.

Answers

E.

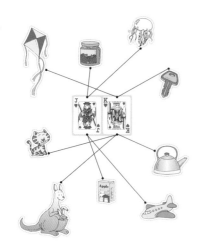

5 Beginning Consonants (3)

A. 1. p   2. m   3. g   4. v
   5. z   6. y   7. n

B.

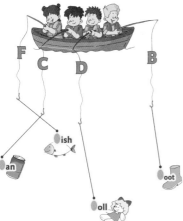

C. 1. s   2. t   3. k   4. h
   5. d   6. l   7. r

D. 1. w   2. r   3. h   4. t
   5. c   6. s   7. j

6 Ending Consonants

A. 1. t   2. d   3. r
   4. b   5. n   6. p

B. 1. t   2. b   3. f
   4. g   5. w   6. l
   7. n   8. p   9. s

C. 1. D ; R   2. K   3. P ; S
   4. G   5. M

D. (Suggested answers)
   1. g ; g ; d   2. n ; n ; t   3. t ; t ; m
   4. r ; r ; n   5. m ; m ; d   6. b ; b ; t
   7. g ; g ; t   8. t ; t ; m   9. d ; d ; n

7 Short Vowel "A"

A. 1. bag   2. cap

   3. fan   4. pan

   5. hat   6. tap

B.

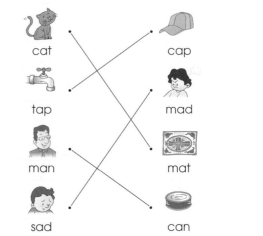

C. 1. B   2. C   3. A   4. D

Smart Practice
   (Suggested answers)
   cab ; cat ; can ; bat ; ban ; tab ; tan ; nab ;
   an ; at ; ant ; act ; a

D. Anna ; hand ; pan ; crab ; mask ; sack ; bat ;
   sand ; Lana

8 Short Vowel "E"

A. 1. e ; E   2. e ; H   3. e ; A
   4. e ; G   5. e ; B   6. e ; F
   7. e ; D   8. e ; C

B. 1. pet   2. well

   3. pen   4. leg

   5. men   6. net

   7. ten **10**   8. bell

C. (In any order)
   wet: set ; get ; bet ; met ; pet ; let

Fred: bed ; wed ; fed ; red ; Ted ; led
yell: cell ; sell ; bell ; well ; fell ; tell

Smart Practice
(Individual writing and drawing)

D.

9 Short Vowel "I"

A. 1. E ; i   2. D ; i   3. B ; i
   4. C ; i   5. A ; i

B. 1. i   2. i   3. i
   4. i   5. i

C.

D. (In any order)
   it: fit ; lit ; pit ; bit ; wit ; sit (Any five)
   hip: lip ; pip ; tip ; rip ; sip ; dip ; zip (Any five)

Smart Practice
   pig ; big ; wig
   (Individual drawing)

10 Short Vowel "O"

A. 4 ; 5 ; 6 ; 7 ; 8 ; 10

B. 1. top   2. pot   3. hot
   4. mop   5. hop

C. 1.   2.

   3.    4.

Smart Practice
(Individual writing and drawing)

D. 1. An ox on a rock   2. Lots of dots
   3. A hopping dog   4. Soft socks

11 Short Vowel "U"

A. 1. B ; u   2. F ; u   3.
   4. D ; u   5. E ; u   6. C ; u
   7. A ; u   8.

B. 1. u   2. u   3. u   4. u
   5. u   6. u   7. u   8. u
   9. u   10. u

C. Ruff, ruff!   Yuck!

 Chuff, chuff!   Run, run as fast as you can.

 Yum, yum!   I'll huff and I'll puff...

Smart Practice
(Individual writing and drawing)

D. 1.   2.

   3.    4.

12 Short Vowels

A. bat ; skunk ; duck ; pig ; hen ; fox ; elephant ; crab ; fish ; frog

B. 1.   2.

   3.   4.

   5.   6.

   7.   8.

C. fox ; rocks
   bat ; hat
   fish ; wish
   clock ; sock
   pet ; jet
   bug ; mug
   hen ; ten
   dog ; jog

Answers

Smart Practice

e ; e ; e

D. (Answers may vary.)

just ; cap ; smell ; win ; dot ; little ; but ; test ;

hill ; fat ; yes ; dish ; fun ; tag

Review 1

A.

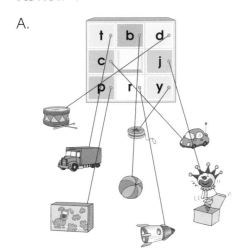

B. 1. ✔   2. ✔   3. ✗
4. ✗   5. ✔   6. ✗
7. ✗   8. ✗   9. ✔

C. 1. g ; s   2. n ; t   3. l ; f
4. w ; l   5. j ; r   6. v ; n
7. s ; k   8. b ; w   9. f ; g
10. m ; p

D. 1. e   2. a   3. i   4. o
5. i   6. a   7. u   8. o
9. e   10. u

E. flag: tag ; bag
well: smell ; tell
fit: mitt ; hit
pin: fin ; chin
fox: box ; ox

F.
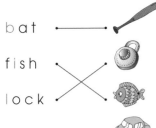
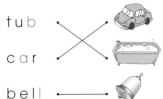

13 Long Vowels / Silent "E"

A.
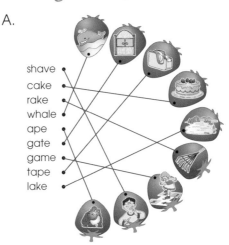

B. 1. fate   2. cape
3. fade   4. hate
5. tape   6. made
7. rate   8. bathe
9. pale   10. ate

C.

D. 1. kite   2. bite   3. pine
4. fine   5. ripe   6. pipe
7. ride   8. hide

E. 1. rope   2. hose   3. robe
4. stone   5. hole

14 More Long Vowels / Silent "E"

A. (Suggested answers)
1. p   2. J   3. r
4. c   5. t   6. m

B. 1. e   2. e   3. e
4. e   5. e   6. e

C. 1. a ; a   2. o   3. o ; o
4. i ; i   5. u ; u   6. i ; i ; i
7. a ; a

D. cone ; rope ; male ; mule ; bake ; fame ;
ride ; rule ; pole ; write

E. A. write   B. globe   C. gate
1. flute   2. nine   3. ice

Smart Practice

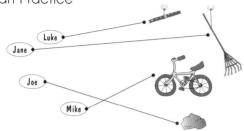

15 Consonant Blends "L"

A. 1. gl   2. sl   3. fl
4. gl   5. fl   6. bl
7. gl   8. cl   9. pl
10. sl   11. cl   12. cl
13. pl   14. bl   15. fl
16. cl

B. 1. oom   2. am   3. ag
4. ove   5. ant   6. ug

C. 1. bl ; cl ; fl   2. bl ; cl ; gl
3. bl ; gl ; sl ; fl (Any three)
4. cl ; sl ; fl   5. cl ; sl ; pl

D. 1.   2.
3.   4.
5.   6.

16 Consonant Blends "R"

A. Brenda ; Fred ; Dreamed ; fresh ; bread ; grabbed ; train ; train ; drove ; crack ; track ; friends ; crumb

B. cr ; br ; gr ; dr

C.

D.
1. dr   2. br   3. tr
4. fr   5. gr   6. cr
7. tr   8. dr   9. br
10. br   11. cr   12. pr

E.
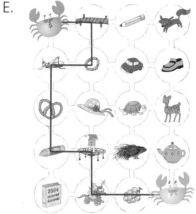

17 Consonant Blends "S"

A. 1. sc   2. sw   3. sc
4. st   5. sn   6. sm
7. sk   8. sp   9. sn

B. 1.   2. 3.   4. 5.   6.

C. 1. in ; in   2. an ; an   3. all ; all
4. ow ; ow   5. y ; y   6. ell ; ell
7. ip ; ip   8. im ; im   9. oop ; oop
10. ill ; ill

D. Circle 1, 2, 3, 4, 5, and 8.

18 Consonant Blends – Review

A.

Answers

B. 1. sk ; pl   2. sl ; sw   3. dr ; pl
    4. st ; br   5. sn ; cl   6. cr ; tr
    7. sl ; sp

C. 2. st ; tr   3. cl ; tr   4. br ; st
    5. pl ; tr   6. cl ; dr   7. fl ; pl
    8. br ; gl   9. sl ; sn   10. sm ; fl

D. (Suggested answers)
    1. fl   2. cl   3. tr
    4. sm   5. fr   6. pl
    7. st   8. bl   9. gr
    10. sc   11. tr   12. fl
    13. cl

19 Consonant Digraphs "CH" and "SH"

A. Check ✔ 2, 5, 6, 7, 8, 10, and 11.

B. 1. sh   2. sh   3. sh
    4. sh   5. sh   6. sh
    7. sh   8. sh   9. sh
    10. sh

C. 1. ch   2. ch   3. sh
    4. sh   5. sh   6. ch
    7. ch   8. ch

D. (Individual drawings and colouring)

Smart Practice
    church

20 Consonant Digraphs "TH" and "WH"

A.

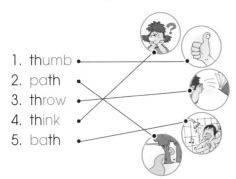

1. thumb
2. path
3. throw
4. think
5. bath

B.

e	o	t	h	e	y	t
m	t	h	o	s	e	a
t	h	e	m	r	t	m
h	a	r	y	e	h	r
e	t	e	t	h	i	s

C. 1. wh   2. wh   3. wh
    4. wh   5. wh   6. wh
    7. wh   8. wh

Smart Practice
    1. When   2. Where   3. Why

D. 1. th   2. wh   3. th
    4. wh   5. th / wh   6. th
    7. wh   8. th   9. wh
    10. wh

E. 1. th   2. wh   3. wh
    4. th   5. wh   6. wh
    7. wh   8. th   9. th
    10. th   11. wh   12. th

21 "ER", "IR", and "UR"

A. ER:
    2. er ;   3. er ;

    4. er ;   5. er ;

    6. er ;

IR:
    1. ir ;   2. ir ;

    3. ir ;   4. ir ;

    5. ir ;   6. ir ;

UR:
    1. ur ;   2. ur ;

    3. ur ;   4. ur ;

5. ur ;   6. ur ;

B. 1.   2.

3.   4.

C. (In any order)
Sir ; Burt ; Bernie ; were ; dirt ; shirt ; hurt ;
water ; squirt

D.

22 Vowel Pair "EE"

A. (Beep)! (Beep)! Said the (jeep).
(Wheels) (peeling) down
the (street)
Hush! Or wake the
(sheep) we (keep).
It's fast (asleep) and
dreaming (sweet).
1. jeep   2. wheels   3. street
4. sheep   5. asleep
B. 1. ee   2. een   3. ee
4. eet   5. eeth   6. eel
7. eet   8. eep   9. eel
10. eet
C. 1.   2.

3.   4.

5.   6.

7.   8.

D. 1. ee ; ee   2. ee ; ee   3. ee ; ee
4. ee ; ee   5. ee ; ee
E. 1. wet   2. bed   3. pear
4. wear   5. pet   6. sell

23 Vowel Pair "OO"

A. kangaroo ; rooster ; raccoon ; baboon ;
cuckoo ; goose ; loon ; moose
1. baboon   2. kangaroo
3. moose   4. rooster
5. raccoon   6. goose
B. 1. B   2. F   3. E   4. G
5. A   6. C   7. D
C. 1. boot   2. moon   3. balloon
4. broom   5. food   6. roof
7. hook   8. wood
D. 1. oop ; oop ; oop
2. ool ; ool ; ool
3. oot ; oot ; oot
4. ook ; ook ; ook
5. oo ; oo ; oo
6. oom ; oom ; oom

24 "Y" as a Vowel

A. 1. rocky   2. curly   3. snowy
4. lady   5. cherry   6. city
7. baby   8. happy   9. sunny
10. jelly   11. starry   12. marry
B. 1. long "i"   2. long "e"
3. long "i"   4. long "i"
5. long "e"   6. long "i"
7. long "e"   8. long "e"
9. long "e"   10. long "i"
11. long "i"   12. long "e"
13. long "i"   14. long "e"
C. 1.   2.

3.   4.

5.   6.

7.   8.

D.

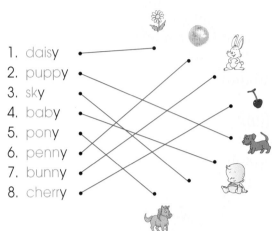

1. daisy
2. puppy
3. sky
4. baby
5. pony
6. penny
7. bunny
8. cherry

Smart Practice

y ; y ; y ; y

Review 2

A. 1. i ; a ; i   2. i ; a   3. a ; u
   4. a ; a   5. i ; o   6. o ; u
   7. u ; u ; i ; u 8. l ; o

B. Colour the ○ with "dr", "sk", "pl", "cr", and "sw".

C. 1. sh   2. th   3. wh
   4. ch   5. sh   6. ch
   7. th   8. wh   9. wh

D. 1. B   2. D   3. H
   4. F   5. A   6. E
   7. G   8. I   9. C

E. 1. ee ; ee 2. oo   3. ee
   4. ee   5. oo   6. oo
   7. ee   8. oo   9. ee

F. Circle these words:
   snowy ; party ; sky ; cry ; dry ; happy ; baby ; try ; celery ; pigsty ; candy ; butterfly
   Long "i":
   sky ; cry ; dry ; try ; pigsty ; butterfly
   Long "e":
   snowy ; party ; happy ; baby ; celery ; candy

Phonics Playground

1

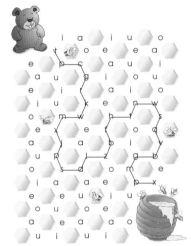

2 1. 2.

   3. 4.

3

4 1. i ;   2. i ;   3. u ;
   4. e ;   5. o ;   6. a ;
   7. o ;   8. a ;   9. u ;

5

tw ice
pl anet
wh ich
sh irt
ch alk
cl oud
th ree
cr ayon
sq uare
br oom

6 (Individual answers)

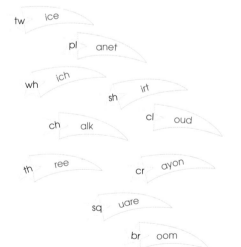